MW00512538

This is
MY STORY.

©The Life Graduate Publishing Group

No part of this book may be scanned, reproduced or distributed in any printed or electronic form without the prior permission of the author or publisher.

ABOUT THE AUTHOR

Name:

Signature

This is my Story

"Mother is the name for God in the
lips and hearts of little children."
— William Makepeace Thackeray

The Beginning.....

Full Name at Birth

_____

Date of Birth   /   /_____

Time of Birth   :_____

Day of the week you were born?_____

Height at birth?_____

Weight at birth?_____

Place of Birth (include City/Town, Country)

_____

Did you have any siblings when you were born? If so, what were their names and their ages?

_____

_____

This is my Story...

Add any additional notes or
information here...

The Beginning.....

Share with us some information about your parents?

_____

_____

_____

_____

_____

What have you been told about you as a baby?

_____

_____

_____

Did you have any unique characteristics or funny things you did as a baby?

_____

_____

_____

_____

This is my Story...

Add any additional notes or
information here...

The Beginning.....

What were your first words?

_____

Were you in good health as a baby?

_____

_____

Do you have any other baby memories to share?

_____

_____

_____

_____

_____

_____

_____

This is my Story...

"The influence of a mother in the lives of her children is beyond calculation."
—James E. Faust

Childhood Years

What was your favorite toy growing up?

_____

_____

Did you have a pet or any pets growing up?

_____

_____

What was your favorite T.V show to watch as a child?

_____

_____

Was there a moment you remember getting into big trouble as a child? Was there a punishment?

_____

_____

_____

_____

_____

_____

This is my Story...

Add any additional notes or information here...

Childhood Years

What are your fondest memories growing up between the ages of 5 years to 12 years?

_____

_____

_____

_____

_____

_____

_____

_____

_____

_____

_____

_____

Add any additional notes or
information here...

Childhood Years

Where did you grow up as a child?
(house,location, town etc)

_____

_____

_____

_____

Who was your best friend or your best friends as a child?

_____

_____

What was your favorite day of the week and why?

_____

_____

_____

_____

This is my Story...

"There is no role in life that is more essential than that of motherhood."
—Elder M. Russell Ballard

Childhood Years

What was your favorite meal as a child?

_____

What elementary/primary school did you attend and where was it located?

_____

_____

Describe your most memorable moment or story from elementary/primary school.

_____

_____

_____

_____

_____

_____

_____

_____

_____

Add any additional notes or information here...

Teenage Years..

Describe your dress sense and clothing as a teenager. Is there anything that stands out for you?

_____

_____

_____

When and where did you learn to drive a vehicle?

_____

_____

What was your first vehicle and how much did you purchase it for? Tell us your special 'first car' story!

_____

_____

_____

_____

_____

_____

_____

_____

Add any additional notes or
information here...

Teenage Years..

Describe your dress sense and clothing as a teenager. Is there anything that stands out for you?

_____

_____

_____

When and where did you learn to drive a vehicle?

_____

_____

What was your first vehicle and how much did you purchase it for? Tell us your special 'first car' story!

_____

_____

_____

_____

_____

_____

_____

Add any additional notes or information here...

Teenage Years..

What High School did you attend and where was it located?

_____

_____

_____

Who was you favorite teacher or coach and why?

_____

_____

_____

What was your favorite subject at school?

_____

_____

Did you date anyone at High School?

_____

_____

_____

This is my Story...

"There is no influence so powerful as that of the mother."
—Sara Josepha Hale

Teenage Years..

What hobbies did you have as a teenager?

_____

_____

What is your most memorable moment as a teenager?

_____

_____

_____

_____

_____

If you knew what you know today, what would you have done differently as a teenager?

_____

_____

_____

_____

_____

This is my Story...

Add any additional notes or information here...

Teenage Years..

Did you have a close friendship group? Have you maintained contact with any of them?

_____

_____

_____

_____

_____

Did you have any nicknames at High School?

_____

_____

What 5 words come to mind to describe your teenage years?

1. _____

2. _____

3. _____

4. _____

5. _____

"A mother's arms are more comforting than anyone else's."
— Princess Diana

When I was .....

When I was a child, my mode of transport to school was..

_____

_____

When I was in my teens, the biggest news story that I recall was .....

_____

_____

_____

When I was growing up, my 3 favorite movies were:

1. _____

2. _____

3. _____

Add any additional notes or information here...

When I was .....

When I was a child, the first movie I went to the theatre to see was..

_____

When I graduated from elementary/primary school, the year was.. _____

When I was 8 years old, I wanted to be a......

_____

When I was 18 years old, my favorite music and band was..

_____

When I was in my teens, the most popular thing to do on a Saturday night was.......

_____

_____

When I was young, I loved to travel to.......

_____

_____

This is my Story...

Family History

My grandparents names were:

Grandmother: _____

Grandfather: _____

They were born in: (country)
Grandmother: _____

Grandfather: _____

This is something that not many people may know about our family history......

_____

_____

_____

_____

_____

Additional Family History information:

_____

_____

_____

This is my Story...

Our FAMILY
──── TREE ────

GrandFather

☐

GrandFather

☐

Grandmother

☐

Grandmother

☐

Mother

☐

Father

☐

Me

☐

"When you look at your mother, you are looking at the purest love you will ever know."
— Mitch Albom

Parenthood

How old were you when you first became a parent?

_____

Explain how you felt emotionally when you bacame a parent for the first time?

_____

_____

_____

_____

_____

Where were you located (city/town/country) when you had your first child?

_____

_____

_____

Add any additional notes or information here...

Parenthood

What has been the biggest challenge for you as a parent?

_____

_____

_____

_____

What are 3 key responsibilities you believe are important as a parent?

1 _____

_____

2 _____

_____

3 _____

_____

This is my Story...

"A mother's happiness is like a beacon, lighting up the future but reflected also on the past in the guise of fond memories."
— Honore de Balzac

Parenthood

Expand on any further parenting memories you may like to share

_____

_____

_____

_____

_____

_____

_____

_____

_____

_____

_____

Add any additional notes or information here...

More about me!

Not many people know this about me, so let me share it with you:

_____

_____

_____

_____

_____

_____

_____

_____

The activity or hobby that I enjoy most to do now is.....

_____

_____

I have the unique ability to be able to....

_____

_____

_____

This is my Story...

Add any additional notes or information here...

More about me!

If I was able to go back to a special time in history, it would be...

_____

_____

_____

If I could pass on one word of advice to others, it would be..

_____

_____

_____

There are special moments in life that you wish you could pause to enjoy for longer. Mine would be......

_____

_____

_____

_____

_____

This is my Story...

"A mother's love is more beautiful than any fresh flower."
— Debasish Mridha

More about me!

I wish I had the opportunity to...

_____

_____

_____

The quote that resonates most with me is..

_____

_____

_____

_____

My favorite book of all time is:

_____

If there is one thing I would like to be remembered for it would be:

_____

_____

_____

This is my Story...

Add any additional notes or
information here...

More about me!

When I look back on my life so far, my 3 proudest moments are:

1 _____

2 _____

3 _____

If there were 3 famous people that I could invite for dinner they would be:

1 _____

2 _____

3 _____

Add any additional notes or
information here...

More about me!

From my teen years, these are the jobs that I've had:

_____

_____

_____

_____

_____

_____

_____

_____

_____

_____

This is my Story...

"A mother's love is everything. It is
what brings a child into this world.
It is what molds their entire being.
When a mother sees her child in
danger, she is literally capable of
anything. Mothers have lifted cars
off of their children and destroyed
entire dynasties. A mother's love is
the strongest energy known to man."
—Jamie McGuire

More about me!

One of the jobs that stands out as my most enjoyable has been..

_____

_____

The most interesting place I have ever traveled to has been.... (include the year/date this occurred)

_____

_____

_____

If I was given a free return flight to anywhere in the world, I would visit...(include your 'Why')

_____

_____

_____

_____

This is my Story...

Final Notes...

There have been many questions that I have answered in this book, but I would also like to share this with you...

Your time to write anything else you wish to share

_____

_____

_____

_____

_____

_____

_____

_____

_____

_____

Final Notes...

Memories

Photos, moments....anything

Memories

Photos, moments....anything

Memories

Photos, moments....anything

Memories

Photos, moments....anything

Memories

Photos, moments....anything

Memories

Photos, moments....anything

Other Books in the series

The Life Graduate
PUBLISHING GROUP

CPSIA information can be obtained
at www.ICGtesting.com
Printed in the USA
LVHW041216011020
667641LV00003B/244

9 781922 453051